Wishbone
Elspeth Smith

Smith/Doorstop Books

Published 2007 by
Smith/Doorstop Books
The Poetry Business
The Studio
Byram Arcade
Westgate
Huddersfield HD1 1ND

Copyright © Elspeth Smith 2007
All Rights Reserved

ISBN 978-1-902382-95-1
Typeset at The Poetry Business
Printed by Swiftprint, Huddersfield

The Poetry Business gratefully acknowledges the help of Arts Council England.

Acknowledgements
Some of these poems first appeared in *The North*.

Contents

5	Wishbone
6	Fancy Dress
7	'At Night'
8	Morning Dormitory
9	Lights Out
10	Retreating
11	Captured
12	Cutting Up
13	Glimpse
13	Minor Character
14	Teddy Bear
14	Same Age
15	Madsummer
15	This Window
16	Curtains
16	Statues
17	Leg
17	Idle Hand
18	Meeting You
18	Bad Luck
19	Going Down
20	Handshake
21	Party
22	New Arrival
22	A Promise
23	Purpose Built
24	Last Invitation
24	Outside

Wishbone

The feast is over.
I am stripped and shining
after the wildest night.
I watched the wine flow,
balloons rise to the roof,
saw the great star
at the top of the tree,
felt every piece of flesh picked from me
as it must be.
I hold a privileged position.
In my brittle brilliance
your fingers take me up.
Your words are secrets in the sky.
Now I am high in your hands.

Wait

Your wish will come true.

Fancy Dress

Will you come as Spring,
All teasing green,
tripping in sweetly
on tiptoeing feet?
Appear as Winter,
freezing white,
icicles dripping
from silver fingers?
Would you be summer,
smothered red,
an invitation
to a bed of roses?
Or risk arriving
undisguised?

'At Night'

You are my lullabies,
my special screw tops.
You are those warm words
on a cold label.
Come with me now,
let me take you altogether.
Slip away with me into mysterious whispers.
You could be the sweetest pills
I ever swallowed.

You rattle happily,
prefer to follow
more sensible directions.

Morning Dormitory

Six neat beds,
counterpanes straightened
like narrow paths
for us to tread.
Six towels
hanging damply
after the freezing strip wash.
Six flannels
wet from faces
craving make up.
Six pairs of slippers
belonging to feet
eager for
vague
wild dancing.

Lights Out

Follow the crocodile of ghosts
to the top of vanished stairs
where sleeping girls are dreaming
of the kiss that will rudely awaken them.
Go to the overgrown garden,
hear old sounds of tennis balls.
Listen to forbidden whispers
in the nights' nine o'clock silence.
Chestnut trees are spreading over
small gym-knickered figures
hanging dutifully upside down,
all in the cause of learning
to be strictly civilized.
Little lost conduct stars
laugh in the grass.

After the fire.

Retreating

I packed my blackest bag.
A fresh brush for my clenched teeth,
a sponge still holding little drops
from familiar taps,
a box of chocolates
for the hungry nights ahead.
Unscented soap
clung smugly to the basin.
Towels were waiting
to dry me up
after my sins were washed away
in all those quantities of hot and cold
wildly running water.
How many was I expected to have committed?
I slipped downstairs.
Escaped again.

Captured

Tonight you will hear new music.
This place will change.
You will make unusual movements,
take strange steps,
speak unfamiliar words.
You came in innocence,
will stay forever
trapped in my pages.

Cutting Up

Now I am closed eyes,
folded hands,
carefully controlled.
I followed pretty patterns,
prepared the way for every stitch,
all those little needles
ran smoothly through the paths I made.
Then my blades began to tremble.
I was tearing at the paper,
slashing at the letters.
I started on the sheets,
the shirts,
the curtains.

I was taken away
with the other sharp possessions.

Glimpse

Leaves concealed it,
thick green summer
keeping the secrets.

Stark branches
bare the truth.

Soon snow will be falling.

Minor Character

What are you doing
in this pretty little present tense,
you with your mad adjectives?
I arranged for you to stay
in that flashback.
These verbs do not concern you now.
The nouns are not yours any more.
Why do you keep returning to me?

Teddy Bear

Your ears have never heard
those words of love.
Your eyes have never seen
this bright white bedroom.
Your mouth will not move
from where it's stitched.
Secrets are safe with you.

Same Age

You must play with others of your own age.
Enjoy your toys together,
make a joyful noise together,
hit each other on your little heads.

You must stick with others of your own age.
Explore the world together,
lead each other
into every way to go astray.

You must stay with others of your own age.
Sit and stare together
at the empty spaces of the day,
prepare to rest in peace together.

Madsummer

Sun is let loose now.
Days dance crazily,
screaming green.
Sky is higher,
bursting blue.
Flowers bloom outrageously
like uncontrolled laughter.
Feet slip from sandals
onto burning ground.

This Window

shows you the tops of those trees,
brings you the sound of those birds
gives you the warmth from that sun,
the light from that moon.
This window
with bars.

Curtains

We have nothing to show you,
nothing to hide.
Your prying eyes
can turn to us.
Look,
there is nothing to see
now.

Statues

Are you waiting
for the music
that suddenly stopped
as you danced
in your garden?

Leg

Waiting for the flames,
a length of skin and bone,
chewed playfully
by some mischievous malignancy.
An elegant shape, death white,
once wild high kicking Can Can black
dizzily fish netted,
catching every necessary eye.
Pale nails, no longer painted,
on toes that tripped
through tempting places.
> That dancing foot
> will bravely take
> this step alone.

Idle Hand

Whose number can I tap tonight?
Who dare I disturb?
Whose turn is it
to suffer?
What can I offer?

I have a little scandal…

Meeting You

I know these eyes
but not these grinning
sticks of teeth,
these hands stretched out to me
like frantic branches.
A winter tree,
how had you danced that summer?

I know these eyes.
They stare at me
from every mirror.

Bad Luck

I sparkled
at all you were told
in the sweet heat
of those odd moments.
My broken bits will bring you the next seven years.

Going Down

Now I belong to diamonds.
Oh Elizabeth,
what have you done?
Taking me to all these
heaven scented, cherished memories,
the red door, the sunflowers, the blue grass?
I splash ecstatically,
I am high
flying,
dabbing, drenching, spraying,
playing a game,
hoping I can pay the price.

I go down
to the safe waters of lavender.

Handshake

Will these fingers keep meeting?
Will something pass
occasionally
between them?
Will they quite cheerfully
wave themselves away?
Will they blow kisses?
Dry tears?
Stroke softly?
Never touch again?

Party

To you
inviting us wildly
into your place of rainbows

and you
spreading the table
with golden eggs

and you
with your silver dreams
reaching your heaven

and you
from your midnight tent
in mysterious mountains

and you
from your sun and sky
and faraway stars

you
who were there
that night

New Arrival

Wait.
It is not yet time to take me
as you took those others,
in your stride.
I am still a closed curtain.
An unopened envelope,
my writing not known to you.
Your folded paper
showing that odd inviting word.
A soft slice of bread
ready for toasting.
Will you fill me
with all your overflowing
or only ignore me,
letting me waste away?
Will I be welcomed,
cherished,
remembered for ever?

A Promise

I am here at last
surrounded by roses,
touching the glass of your window.
I peer
into an empty room.

Purpose Built

You sleep on my forgotten footsteps.
Do I disturb your dreams?
By tripping across
old pieces of bricks and mortar
when the sun was hot
on the top of my life
and your place
was a space in the sky

waiting for you?

Last Invitation

Come.
I am covered with flowers,
exquisitely polished,
ready to perish
in fire or earth.
Come to me breathlessly.
Need nothing more.

Outside

Here is the gate,
waiting.
Here is the open door,
the windows
sparkling.
This is the house
I must never enter.
This is the bell
I must never ring.